CORONAVIRUS HAIKU

Cover design by Faride Mereb
Cover art by Sabine Bitter
Interior composition by Patrick Durgin
Set in Akzidenz-Grotesk and Minion

ISBN: 978-1-7343176-4-0
Library of Congress Control Number: 2021931999

Published by Kenning Editions

Kenningeditions.com

Distributed by Small Press Distribution
1341 Seventh St., Berkeley, CA 94710

Spdbooks.org

This book was made possible in part by the supporters of Kenning Editions:
Alan Bernheimer, Jay Besemer, Mark Booth, Joel Craig, Ian Dreiblatt, Joseph
Giardini, Katherine M. Hedeen, Krystal Languell, Joslyn Layne, Olivia Lott,
Pamela Lu, Olivia DiNapoli, Thomas Troolin, and The John A. Hartford
Foundation.

Kenning Editions is a 501c3 non-profit, independent literary publisher
investigating the relationships of aesthetic quality to political commitment.
Consider donating or subscribing: Kenningeditions.com/shop/donation

CORONAVIRUS HAIKU

WORKER WRITERS SCHOOL

EDITED BY MARK NOWAK

CHICAGO: KENNING EDITIONS: 2021

Table of Contents

Introduction by Mark Nowak   9

Coronavirus Haiku

    Alando McIntyre   23

    Alfreda Small   31

    Christine Lewis   34

    Davidson Garrett   40

    Doreen McGill   46

    Estabon Chimilio   51

    Kelebohile Nkhereanye   54

    Kerl Brooks   57

    Lorraine Garnett   61

    Nimfa Despabiladeras   70

    Paloma Zapata   73

    Seth Goldman   77

    Thomas Barzey   85

Contributors   90

Introduction | 9

When the coronavirus pandemic first began its lethal decent upon New York City and countries across the globe in the first months of 2020, the Worker Writers School (WWS) was just beginning to plan for the celebration of its first decade providing free poetry workshops to members of worker centers, trade unions, and other working-class community organizations. The writers in this anthology hail from our worker center partners in New York City including Domestic Workers United, New York Taxi Workers Alliance, Damayan Migrant Workers Association, Street Vendor Project, and Retail Action Project. Additionally, our past collaborators – Haitian Women for Haitian Refugees, Picture the Homeless, Worker Justice Center of New York, National Council on Occupational Safety and Health, and other organizations in New York, as well as Justice for Domestic Workers (now The Voice of Domestic Workers) in London, Indonesian Migrant Workers Union in Amsterdam and The Hague, NUMSA (National Union of Metalworkers of South Africa) in Port Elizabeth and Pretoria, and other trade unions – have also deeply impacted this "new history" of poetry practice that we have been developing in our workshops, public events, and publications.[1]

I remember like few others the day WWS workshop participants began discussing and writing "coronavirus haiku." On March 7, 2020, a sunny and unseasonably warm late winter Saturday (the WWS workshops always meet at

---

[1] As Cedric Robinson keenly notes in the concluding chapter of his monumental study, *Black Marxism: The Making of the Black Radical Tradition*, "For the realization of a new theory we require a new history." My use of "new history" is drawn from this context and the larger "new history" I outline in *Social Poetics*. Cedric J. Robinson, *Black Marxism: The Making of the Black Radical Tradition* (Chapel Hill: University of North Carolina Press, 2000 [1983]), 307.

PEN America on the first Saturday of the month), stories about a new global virus were just beginning to permeate the news. In the days leading up to our workshop, Vice President Mike Pence publicly revealed that nineteen crew members and two passengers aboard the Grand Princess cruise ship, which was returning to California from Hawai'i, had tested positive for the virus and that all 3,500 passengers on the ship were required to quarantine in their cabins.[2] In New York, another story announced a "sudden jump in positive results – from one on Sunday to eleven by Wednesday" and mentioned that the first case had been found in New Jersey, "a man in his 30s who had been hospitalized since Tuesday."[3] None of us had any idea on that day what the coming weeks and months had in store.

We did not come to writing coronavirus haiku as novices on that first Saturday in March. Members of the WWS had spent the previous six months in the "social world of study," as Fred Moten and Stefano Harney have called the kind of practice we engage in, of a more radical tradition of the haiku.[4] Our work with haiku started in September 2019 when acclaimed Japanese translator and critic Hiroaki Sato – author of a recently published book, *On Haiku* – led a haiku workshop at our fall assembly at the People's Forum, "Study Hall: Radical Study and Stuart Hall."[5] Sato's

---

[2] Thomas Fuller, Sarah Mervosh, Tim Arango, and Jenny Gross, "21 Coronavirus Cases on Cruise Ship Near California," https://www.nytimes.com/2020/03/06/us/california-coronavirus-cruise-ship.html.

[3] Michael Gold and Luis Ferré-Sadurni, "9 New Cases of Coronavirus in N.Y., All Connected to Westchester Man," https://www.nytimes.com/2020/03/04/nyregion/coronavirus-nyc-yeshiva-university.html.

[4] Stefano Harney and Fred Moten, *The Undercommons: Fugitive Planning & Black Study* (Wivenhoe, U.K.: Minor Compositions, 2013), 109.

[5] "Study Hall: Radical Study + Stuart Hall" was part of a series of assemblies the Worker Writers School has been convening annually on Governor's Island and at The People's Forum, a new social movement incubator space in NYC's garment district. The assembly in 2019 where Sato led a workshop also included a panel on radical study with William Ayers and Eli Meyerhoff as well as a conversation on Stuart Hall with Ruth Wilson Gilmore (moderated by Nicole Fleetwood). For more details on the September event, see https://www.facebook.com/events/2331744640228496/. Guests at our previous WWS assemblies have included Patricia Smith, Vijay Prashad, Joy James, John Keene, Fred Moten, Stefano Harney, and many others.

workshop handout introduced writers from the WWS to a wide range of haiku practitioners: Richard Wright, Nakamura Kusatao, Jack Kerouac, ai li, Mishima Yukio, and others. Although Sato is a proponent of "monolinear haiku" in his translation practice – "I must make it clear that the lineation of poems in translation is my hobby horse, and that I regard the haiku as basically a one-line poem and translate it accordingly," as he writes in *On Haiku* – the examples on his handout included predominantly three-line versions like those collected here.[6] During his afternoon workshop, Sato stressed irreverence in haiku; these seventeen-syllable poems should engage themes such as sex, labor, politics, the body. *They should be not the smoke, but the fire* – that was how I summarized his presentation in my notes. At the end of Sato's workshop, participants from the WWS read drafts of the new haiku they had written that afternoon.

A few weeks later, after work on a Friday in early October, WWS members boarded a bus outside PEN America and travelled to the Berkshires for a weekend writers' retreat. The next morning, we read poems by Basho and Issa beside a mill stream and wrote haiku inspired by this new geography in the landscape where the Shakers had once made their home.[7] Afterwards, participants warmed themselves around the fireplace and read the "Combahee River Collective Statement" and other sections of Keeanga-Yamahtta Taylor's *How We Get Free: Black Feminism and the Combahee River Collective* (a book they had been given when they arrived at the retreat center). Unbeknownst to the retreat participants, Barbara Smith was driving down from Albany at the same time; she would spend half of Saturday with us, sharing her experiences co-writing the Combahee statement, running Kitchen Table: Women of Color Press, and talking about the importance of writing and publishing and organizing walking hand in hand. Christopher Funkhouser came to the retreat center and recorded our evening workshop session where each participant read new poems that would later air on his radio show on WGXC, a regional community

---

[6] Hiroaki Sato, *On Haiku* (New York: New Directions, 2018), 65.

[7] See Stephen J. Stein, *The Shaker Experience in America: A History of the United Society of Believers* (New Haven, Yale University Press, 1994).

radio station.[8] And on the last morning of our retreat, poet and small press publisher Joseph Bruchac visited from his home in the Adirondacks and led us through a workshop that inspired us to write about our ancestors, the landscape, and our stories of displacement and reconnection. Nimfa Despabiladeras, I remember, wrote a particularly heartrending poem about the murder of her grandfather in that workshop. Echoes from all these retreat sessions can be heard in the haiku collected here.[9]

In the winter months between our workshops with Hiroaki Sato, Barbara Smith, and Joseph Bruchac and that first coronavirus haiku writing workshop in early March 2020, WWS members diligently read, analyzed, discussed, and wrote from the inspirations of a more radical haiku tradition: Japanese-American internment camp haiku, haiku of the Black Arts Movement (Sonia Sanchez, Etheridge Knight, Amiri Baraka's "low coup," and haiku from Celes Tisdale's anthology *Betcha Ain't: Poems from Attica*), as well as modernist haiku collected in Makoto Ueda's *Modern Japanese Haiku: An Anthology*. By providing writers in the WWS workshop with a vast tableaux of both 20th-century Japanese poets and a more radical US tradition of haiku practice, we sought to discover and establish a "new history" in our social study and social practice of the haiku form.

We grew to love the haiku as "charged language," as Christine Lewis calls it; as "a punch line," as Lorraine Garnett dubbed it in one interview; and as a gut punch, too. Edward Hirsch, in his definition of the haiku in *A Poet's Glossary*, claims that the Japanese poetic form "seeks the momentary and the eternal," though I'm partial to the more gritty passages that Hirsch quotes from R. H. Blythe who states that a haiku "is an open door that looks shut;" Blythe also points to the haiku's "self-effacing, self-annihilative nature."[10] Hiroaki Sato stresses the haiku's grassroots, anti-

---

[8] The entire episode is archived at https://wavefarm.org/radio/wgxc/schedule/13983r.

[9] Funding for the retreat was made possible by the Vilcek Foundation. The Worker Writers School graciously thanks Vilcek and PEN America for their help in making this retreat possible.

[10] Edward Hirsch, *A Poet's Glossary* (Boston and New York: Houghton Mifflin Harcourt, 2014), 272-73.

enlightenment intensification of language. In one of his early critical volumes, *One Hundred Frogs: From Renga to Haiku to English*, Sato writes that haiku, too long associated with Zen (especially in the USA), are instead written "to congratulate, to praise, to describe, to express gratitude, wit, cleverness, disappointment, resentment, what have you, but rarely to convey enlightenment."[11] And Thomas Rimer, in the introduction to *From the Country of Eight Islands: An Anthology of Japanese Poetry* (a book we also used poems from in our workshop), points to the working-class roots of many of the form's practitioners, stating that "the authors of the poems range from emperors and priests to anonymous soldiers and peasants."[12] This working-class and peasant tradition has also been thoroughly discussed in anthologies edited and translated by Makoto Ueda, as I discuss in *Social Poetics*.[13]

When I walked to PEN America's offices in SoHo on that fateful Saturday in March, I began to toss around in my head this grisly new word that had only recently entered our vocabulary: *Coronavirus, COVID, Covid-19, co-ro-na-vi-rus*. As I repeated each syllable of the word out loud, I realized that the term we were using to name this global pandemic had five syllables and thus could serve as a single line, i.e., either the first or final line, in the haiku's 5-7-5 syllable structure. In that moment, I overhauled what I had planned to use as a writing prompt in our workshop that afternoon. As soon as I arrived at PEN's third floor office, I made myself a cup of PG Tips and began to set up the back room for our workshop. Shortly after I arrived, members of New York City's worker centers began to ring the bell outside the office's front door: nannies, eldercare workers, licensed day-care providers, and others from Domestic Workers United, the organization that struggled to pass the first domestic workers' "Bill of

---

[11] Hiroaki Sato, *One Hundred Frogs: From Renga to Haiku to English* (New York & Tokyo: Weatherhill, 1983), 126-131.

[12] Thomas Rimer, "Introduction," in *From the Country of Eight Islands: An Anthology of Japanese Poetry*, edited and translated by Hiroaki Sato and Burton Watson (Seattle: University of Washington Press, 1981), xxix.

[13] Mark Nowak, *Social Poetics* (Minneapolis: Coffee House Press, 2020), 126-28, 193-94.

Rights" that was signed into law by Governor Patterson in 2010; taxi drivers from the New York Taxi Workers Alliance; current and former members of the Retail Action Project and Damayan Migrant Workers Association; an MTA subway worker from the Street Vendor Project; and others.[14] Audre Lorde and James Baldwin posters on PEN's office walls reminded us that we would be merging working life with writing life for the next two hours.

Typically, when members of the WWS arrive, we greet each other as family: warm hugs, updates on our daily and family lives over the past month since we last met, jokes and jibes (particularly from Seth, a taxi driver), a gentle unpacking of bodies from coats and settling in around a workshop table covered with bananas and clementines, plantain chips, pretzels, cookies, and Hershey's kisses. As people settle into their seats around the table, I take requests for warm drinks: *Coffee with two sugars and a lot of cream! Rooibos Chai, one sugar. Black coffee please. Just water for me, thanks. Mojito Mint Tea, my dear, but I've brought my own honey!* But on March 7, 2020, we greeted each other much differently. Instead of handshakes and hugs, I stood at the glass front door of PEN America's office with a 64 oz. bottle of Purell hand sanitizer. As members of the WWS entered, each person received two firm pumps. Some people giggled about the unexpected new greeting, but everyone understood the reason behind it.

When we were all fully hand-sanitized and unpacked, tea or coffee in hand, conversation immediately turned to Covid-19. Just that day, as I learned after the workshop, Gov. Andrew Cuomo had declared a "State of Emergency" in New York State as cases rose to eighty nine, including an Uber driver in Queens and an outbreak in Westchester County; the *New York Times* article noted that "more than 380 cases of the virus had been confirmed" in the United States, a number that seems unbelievably miniscule now, ten months later, when deaths top 4,000 a day.[15] Workshop

---

[14] See Meaghan Winter, "A Nannies' Bill of Rights," *Slate*, https://slate.com/human-interest/2010/04/a-bill-of-rights-for-domestic-workers-in-new-york.html.

[15] Jesse McKinley and Edgar Sandoval, "Coronavirus in N.Y.: Cuomo Declares State of Emergency," *New York Times*, https://www.nytimes.com/2020/03/07/nyregion/coronavirus-new-york-queens.html.

participants' concerns, not yet fully bloomed, germinated beneath the words we shared that day. I told everyone what I had discovered on my walk to our workshop: the word coronavirus had five syllables and thus could serve as the entire first or last line of a traditional 5-7-5 haiku. *So, let's try to write a "coronavirus haiku" that captures how we are feeling as taxi drivers, nannies, workers in New York City. What have you seen? What are your hopes and fears? Let's take ten-minutes or so to write, and then we'll discuss what we've come up with and end our workshop early today given everything that's going on. We want to keep ourselves safe and healthy.* And thus began our practice of analyzing and writing poems about the global pandemic. After we shared what we had written, we re-packed our bags, put our coats back on again, and posed for the obligatory monthly WWS workshop group photo next to the front reception desk. Everyone would later share, like, and comment on it on social media. Little did we know then that this would be the last time we would see each other in person for a very long time.

March 7, 2020 at PEN America. Left to Right: Alando McIntyre, Kelebohile Nkhereanye, Alfreda Small, Mark Nowak, Nimfa Despabiladeras, Marcia Rose, Christine Lewis, Lorraine Garnett (seated), Seth Goldman, Thomas Barzey, Doreen McGill, Davidson Garrett, Nelson Estabon Chimilio. Photo © Christine Lewis.

To be honest, the next few weeks are a blur for me. I remember sending my wife photos of empty grocery store shelves. I was glued to the news as we began mask wearing and social distancing that we never imagined would still be the way we would be living a year later. When schools and what came to be deemed "non-essential" workplaces closed, many people turned to tools like Facetime and Zoom to work, learn, and at least stay digitally connected to families and friends. And so it was with everyone in our workshop group. I sent an email out to all the WWS members in late March to inform them that our workshop on April 4, 2020, would be held on Zoom (it was all so new to us then!). To my surprise and delight, as I clicked the button to let everyone enter the Zoom workshop from the "waiting room," I could see the joy and relief on everyone's faces that we were still able to gather to write on the first Saturday of the month. In fact, everyone so enjoyed that first online haiku workshop and the momentary return to "normalcy" that participants asked if we could begin meeting twice per month on Zoom – "something to look forward to," a few people said. For the rest of April, the rest of the spring, and the entire summer, we got together on Zoom twice a month to build solidarity and write the coronavirus haiku that are included in this anthology. We read and discussed Diane di Prima's haiku as well as Sato's translations of Fukushima nuclear disaster haiku that were published in *So Happy to See Cherry Blossoms: Haiku from the Year of the Great Earthquake and Tsunami*. We even had a Zoom visit in our November 2020 workshop from Evie Shockley who discussed her "Statistical Haiku" (and the influence of Langston Hughes's "Johannesburg Mines" on her poem). Shortly after Shockley's visit, the poets collected here sent in the haiku they had been writing since March to be considered for publication in this anthology. From one writer alone I received nearly 200 haiku to choose from!

How do the day jobs of frontline or essential workers and a writing practice of haiku come together during a global pandemic? Kelebohile Nkhereanye, originally from Lesotho, wrote a series of five haiku as a way to decompress from and critically analyze her harrowing shift behind the plexiglass booth at one of New York City's subway stations. In one haiku, she tries to tell passengers they are misplacing the blame: "Stress riding the subway/Questions without answers/Not workers fault." In another haiku, she points to the extreme stress of her job: "Emotional violence is present/You need to work/But people humiliate you."

Nimfa Despabiladeras, a domestic worker from the Philippines, wakes up one morning during the pandemic with a morose epiphany: "Boiling water/at 6:00 a.m.," she writes in her haiku, "I realize that/my bird clock is dead." Lorraine Garnett, a domestic worker originally from Jamaica, sketches the early days of uncertainty as well as the unrelenting march of the natural world as coronavirus hangs over the conclusion of a bleak winter. Her haiku fuses themes from classical haiku writers like Buson and Issa with the current moment as the narrator waits for the results of a Covid test. "Missed first day of spring," she writes. "Positive or negative/cherry blossom looms."

The haiku is compact. It jabs and jolts. Some haiku writers stick to the traditional 5-7-5 syllable structure while others experiment, upending the confines of the strict syllable count while sticking to the core idea of the haiku as a 3-line detonation of image and energy. You can write a haiku in a matter of seconds, we learned, though you might keep revising it for months or even years. It takes its language from the streets, from conversation, from the news, from everywhere. Shiki, the pseudonym of Masaoka Noboru, one of the leaders of the haiku reform movement in Japan in the late 1800s and early 1900s, sought a more expansive vocabulary for the haiku. As Shiki wrote in an article for *Nippon* in 1896, "We abhor trite motifs…we do not mind using the vocabulary of ancient court poetry or of modern vernacular slang, or words loaned from Chinese or western languages, as long as the words harmonize with the tone of the haiku."[16]

Seth Goldman, who has been driving New York City's iconic yellow taxis for over thirty-five years, likes to write an earthy, political haiku. He might scribble down a few thoughts while paused at a red light or riding the A Train home after a twelve-hour shift. His cab, he says, has been empty more frequently since coronavirus shuttered so much of NYC.

---

[16] Quoted in Makoto Ueda's introduction to his edited volume *Modern Japanese Haiku: An Anthology* (Toronto: University of Toronto Press, 1976), 5.

After he returns home from work, while chopping onions and garlic as he cooks dinner, he might revise those notes into a seventeen-syllable haiku that speak to how coronavirus has made us rethink our relationship to life's necessities and to time itself: "Clean leather or fur?/Chris French Cleaners on Ninth St./Maybe next winter."

Alando McIntyre joined our workshops as he was nearing the end of an eleven-year run working behind the counter at a Golden Krust bakery in Brooklyn. Christine Lewis, Secretary/Cultural Outreach Coordinator at DWU who has been with our workshop since its inception, started up a conversation with Alando while waiting on her take-out order at the Caribbean restaurant. Now a public school teacher in New York and a regular member of the WWS, Alando tracks the vicissitudes of life during the pandemic and inscribes a small summons to the spirits: "Gave it all up, to fall/Prey, but a new day rises./A round of peace please."

Tom Barzey, whose haiku conclude this volume, is a coronavirus survivor. Members of the WWS remember those late spring and early summer Zoom sessions when Tom first returned after missing several workshops. *I had it*, Tom says into our Zoom screens, *I had the virus. And man, for a while there I didn't think I was gonna make it.* When Tom returned to our workshop, his energy was still low. But as he says, our haiku workshops on Zoom created a space beyond the virus for him, a space to be creative as he thankfully recovered. From what he calls his "aroma" from the lack of showering while sick with Covid and his fear of going outside once he'd begun to recover ("Can't let anyone know me/Please hide me") to the economic effects in his neighborhood ("Ghostly Bronx Town Mall"), Tom documents one life, his life, that survived a virus that has, as of this writing, killed more than 400,000 people in the United States and more than two million people worldwide.

The poems published here stand as a testament to the effects of Covid-19 on the essential workers who have risked their lives to save ours. Yet this volume also stands as testimony to the freedom dreams of these same essential workers in the city that first felt the tidal wave of the virus. And while we now have these coronavirus haiku to read, discuss, admire, and learn from, the larger test of our humanity will no doubt lie in the actions we take when we remember the frontline and essential workers who tried to protect us, nourish us, care for us, heal us, and keep us safe and alive throughout this pandemic. Will we return to former times when we failed to join in the great social struggles for living wages, health care for all, a clean climate, and a sustainable future? Or will we help accelerate the push to dismantle a capitalist system that allowed a few to grossly profit while so many of the rest of us merely tried to survive? Will we recommit to the struggle for not the possibility but rather the inevitability of that "another world" we have chanted for in the streets? Grace Lee Boggs once noted the necessary contribution from cultural workers to this struggle: "...we need artists to create new images that will liberate us from our preoccupations with constantly expanding production and consumption and open up space in our hearts and minds to imagine and create another America that will be viewed by the world as a beacon rather than as a danger."[17] This country has been a space of danger for far too long, for its entire history, in fact, including its sordid history during this global pandemic. But in these coronavirus haiku, new histories and new images render another kind of future, a future of new possibilities and new solidarities, both legible and near at hand.

—Mark Nowak

---

[17] Grace Lee Boggs (with Scott Kurashige), *The Next American Revolution: Sustainable Activism for the Twenty-First Century* (Berkeley: University of California Press, 2011), 36-37.

Coronavirus Haiku

Backroom frolicking,
A gentle kiss from Rona Vi
our modern war play.

Alternative Life –
gloves, body-bags, face masks
crown Corona king!

Lies and truths converge
as unburied bodies roam
Corona City.

Humming of drones
and wailing of sirens can't
keep sunlight away.

Cap! Isms imploding,
sirens scream louder than Bach,
Co-vid freedoms: whack!

In Covid War: I
sip absolute lawlessness,
love with gloves and mask.

Stimulus Package
Can't buy the acre nor the mule.
Oh our pow'r wanes.

Cars zoom across Linden
Blvd. Scene's not popular
on streaming sites.

decluttering truth
reveals plantation living
existing en mask.

Cho! Evry-badi
under house arrest because
of covid!

Man pon bicycle,
radio blaring song from
mi likkle-boy days.

Let's talk bout freedom
while celery juice digests
and ginger tea cools.

Sitting by table
wondering how I became
a pawn for Steve Jobs.

white privilege flails
peculiar thing like the sun
shinning in night sky.

Mailman drops package
like hot potato. We dropped
our rights to dissent.

Government sanctions
kill many without blood flow —
day moon type a vibes.

Two benjis plus
3 dimes and a nickel shot
dead/lynched by the badge.

Fronting like it ain't
bout looks, and pleasing of the
eyes, vase holds dead rose.

The rapture began
not how we expected; saints
sent home by co-vid.

daring to deal with
dregs at the bottom of my
mug of unstrained coffee

The Feds stole our minds while
we tripped on hope and fear.
Still no stars in noon sky.

homelife and worklife
blend kinda rough like mi green
juice, drink but don't taste.

They descended ships
while we remain in holds
still wearing the mask.

with all the black lives
matterin, santa's still white
in the commercials.

Cashier adds up food
Really tired of people
Tulips blooming outside

People in face masks
Gloves hang loose on bony hands
Can't wait to be done

Ferry boat sailing
Crowd rushes to terminal
Subway too nasty

Raisin in the milk
Why I have to say hello
Not welcome in neighborhood

Want to sail away
Warm sun hitting my dry face
Buds bloom near window

Ate taco dinner
Stood on pantry line long time
Hot sun shone on me

Changes to 4 Train
Took forever to get home
Tired as hell now

rats, human vie for
space on urban sidewalk cracks
in tenement walls

broken woman beg
change, sanitary napkin
a first! Wall Street next

melancholy days
stench of death, pungent, linger
U-Haul for a morgue

amidst naked shelves
his lips stained with first milk shout,
"te amo, mami"

dismal Season. then
I am reminded seeds sprout
from cracks in concrete

contrary days, stress
fingers pen sad notes, logged six,
slippery treadmill

4 blocks empty, a
bitch tied to one wrist, summer
madness on repeat

she navigate folks
in mask, subway, madam rooms
for less than fifteen

October fierce purge
leaves, roots, remain decompose
3c fourth floor reeks

brown women warm cold
bench, intersection of dreams
a train below groan

5 am dew, mist
robust rats rake brittle bins
a silent cat sit

Bangladeshi men
deliver tacos, bitter
days, upper east side

November wind loot
listless leaves, boughs of ash, birch
a dog in heat pant

balance madam home,
dust pan, dust cloth, less than 15 now,
American bread

hawk knitted caps, Mark Kay, DKNY
etched in hoodies, daisy dukes.
Pigeons in formation shit on broken leaves

north Station plaza, above frigid railroad
7 am housekeepers huddle, our Lady
of Guadalupe amulet hung from middle finger

empty taxi cabs
cruising along avenues
with bankrupt drivers

corona virus
an invisible culprit
foiled by Clorox

no opera now
the virus darkened the Met
but birds sing to me

tired hot dog vendor
drops huge mustard jar from cart
yellowing sore feet

early morning fog
covers the town like a shroud
death floats in the air

Broadway shows shutdown
Times Square restaurants suffer
thousands of jobs lost

day driver starts shift
chicken bones left on cab's seat
by night driver slob

starving cabdriver
gobbles provolone cheese
taxi smells like feet

time for coffee break
cabbie double parks by store
a cop tickets him

an old cabdriver
pees beside his parked taxi
gold showers bathe curb

skyscrapers asleep
Manhattan midnight eerie
the moon keeps safe watch

grim news on TV
a breeze blows through my window
death chokes the airwaves

taxi drivers hurt
few fares during pandemic
pray no suicides

haughty Hudson Yards
closed down by the pandemic
Neiman Marcus squalls

I lounge in night clothes
in the middle of the day
quarantine fashion

radiator clanks
in my teeny-weenie flat
autumn has arrived

Gulf Coast hurricanes
warnings from Doctor Fauci
President Trump golfs

white supremacists
hate to don masks for safety
prefer Klan hoodies

Met a nanny outside
Why you workin? Better money to close!
Just can't leave mine unattended

Day 1 in March Decided not to close
You fool, You fool, All I heard
Folks got no integrity!

My kids are very young
Covid didn't make them come undone
Simply didn't like mask wearing

My moms were really scared
Travel to work is essential
MTA lost very many!

Lots of gun violence near
Cop told me don't worry. It's everywhere
Only goin to Gristedes at night

Everyone lookin for therapy
Everyone talkin at me
Class has disappeared

Cops cops cops galore
More crime or extreme paranoia
Domestic violence New York

Newyorkafornia. Love you now
So glad I had my windows cleaned
If I could only enjoy the nights

Broadway useta love me
I useta love Broaday
What's Broadway?

What a difference a day makes
Someone sang that song
Now I'm singin it!

I'm feeling great
Haven't slept in a month of Sundays
Harlem bound when this is over

Life is simply good
Wouldn't change anything if I could
Say it! Knock on wood

The sun is bright and strong
just like everyone in NYC today
Even the police are happy

Black hooded white man,
Waiting late night for an Uber
Cops left him alone.

2020 creeps
Forcing its way for all time
Savings time behind.

Highest per 100,000
The Bronx still suffers, Covid.
Break this news before we go.

COVID train riding
My nerves shaking like the rails.
Can't wait to leap off.

Facemask cover-up space
Fear winding down from the rage.
Safe to go jogging again?

No more trick or treat
Yearly street walking, cancelled
Sour taste in my mouth.

Leaves Fall Different
Concrete muffles its beauty
Still I watch, still.

Flies are hovering
Trained by the President's lies
Life cycle nears end.

No cash in the book
No service from 1:00-5:00 a.m.
Full moonlight locally

It is not easy
COVID-19 in the subway
Isolation and trauma

23% blacks in the workplace
Need to sue for advancement
Enjoy fall's yellows, ambers, orange

Use vending machines
No passengers in subways
Full moonlight yesterday

Anger provoked at work
Gender-based violence
Men need to stop

Stress riding the subway
Questions without answers
Not workers fault

270 is your magic
You made the rules
Time for pumpkin pie

November 7, 2020 brought peace
New chapter, new president
Time to clean leaf piles

Morning comes later
I awoke to darkness
No passion to start my day.

On the street
Wind orchestra plays on
Vibrant ballerina spins.

Unpresidential times
This life lived online.
Work, play, grieve, stay.

I take a knee
On another's neck, no
In humility to Authority.

Three a.m. starting time
Bake, serve, meeting of friends
Night, clients still, ends, begins.

Rats, not mouse, bravely strolls
Across these wooden floors of old
Even cats are on unemployment I'm told.

Beautiful monarchs
Fly south before winter comes
Commit suicide via auto.

Ride home interrupted
Food truck lined up blindsided
Seafood, flavored ice dinner.

Eyes on Election
Different numbers rising
Coronavirus 116,707 new.

Over the fence
Once filled with childish laughter
Overgrown grass sways.

On Interstate South
Mid-afternoon traffic speeding
Metal meets concrete divide

Today's new normal
Looking towards Thanksgiving
Zoom family dinner.

Missed first day of spring
positive or negative
cherry blossom looms

Lash to the forehead
open processing meat plants
start cotton picking

Gates open, wealth leads
10 million bucks – jackpot
mom, pop shops collapse

Jailed with corona
thousand dollars bail money
paper towel wipe

Bondage – forced to write
haikus keep me from gasping
chewing black ink pen

Ten days brick labor
lumbar – pothole stabbing pain
paycheck – bounce, bounce twice

Enlist – forced open
frontline – returned to action
hair, nail, ball – riots…

Cheaper – Beijing made
reagents in Mexico
cotton swabs, come home

Just need sun moment
swept up bread crumbs – concrete floor
shared cornmeal fish fry

Saved by the haiku
afraid – museum bedroom
what if bones are found?

Hospital rooms – shrines
doctors, nurses wearing white
final words – faced time

Disposable cups
paper plate, evil hearts kill
black and white rainbow

Careers changing
Respiratory therapist – same
Nurse – Undertaker

Stimulus action
social distance injustice
kicked, whipped, cuffed, then – poof…

Black blood on white sheet
bird season – black birds only
mother hen grief tweets

murder on asphalt
Minnesota crushed cockroach
blood morph word – "mama!"

sorry you're frightened
when will you apologize
for Jim/Karen's laws?

terrorizing streets
white bodies on black bodies
bloody, bloody moon

Open freezer door
dive for Atlantic Ocean
missed – landed in hell

Young black man jogging
two white men hunting – blood sports
spring a trap – three shots

running black bodies
seeking sunlight – few blind eyes
tear gas turned dark clouds

Listening to dogs bark
sirens howling, fireflies
the dog walker died

Rainbow is lurking
rattlesnakes hibernate – rejoice
solitary ends

wailing moral pain
broken heart streams tie-dye blood
epsom salt shower

was thinking we should
stop driving – but – they would get
us for jaywalking

Sweet banana bread
chokehold, knee, rope, bullets, lies…
where is the sugar?

Election stolen?
you took butter – left the knife
People – "We're Speaking!"

Boiling water
At 6:00 a.m., I realize that
my bird clock is dead.

Today, Central Park
playground gate padlocked, empty
swing sways in the breeze.

Crowded hospitals with
body bags in freezer trucks
disposed in shallow graves.

Street sweeper cleans on Monday
Honking loudly at parked cars
Stubborn folks don't care.

Opened kitchen lights.
Saw a bug: swat!
The fly got away.

First time I saw
A homeless man
Smile at me in a while.

There's word going around.
Prepare yourself: stock your pantries.
Fear of election outcome: violence.

…two haiku in memory of Arlena Juanico

Covid 19 took
A mother away, her kid
Waits for her return

No way to explain
No more hugs and no more kisses
Now: just ashes

ok, key, wallet, mask
stay away, too close, hold that train!
S*** I forgot the milk

a straight road ahead
to the ant hills and valleys
one step forward counts

the cashier looks numb
scanning items like frozen goods
hot days beg for you

Sore, buzzing, hot
not enough ideas see the light
blank, silent, stiff

Time lifts away, dissolves
numbers flying spinning 'round
empty face leads long nights

pickles and French fries
two bees buzzing, it's a fight
printmaking begins

Look homemade cookies!
check for more, November score
not enough, the line stops

Inner city woes
Flee to the woods for fresh air
Lockdown loves panic

Scrolling words and bombs
no surprises in 2020
the last leaf dances

I question myself
how did I get here? when? why?
guess it's winter again

Clean leather or fur?
Chris French Cleaners on Ninth St.
Maybe next winter

The Crabbie Cabbie
Now an essential worker
May God bless us all

$2.50 an hour
Corona Cabbie Wages
April 15 looms

Strong April Showers
Will bring Cabbies dead flowers
Workers, not Wall St.

So isolating
Cabbing down Broadway today
The wind screams Mary

Covid-19 Days
Imaginary beer friends
I drink ale alone

9 hours empty
A 12-hour taxi shift
Spent 6 with Basie

Made 4 bucks an hour
Spent 60 on groceries
Will eat 'til I'm sick

Call unemployment?
Relief for taxi worker$?
Pick up the FUCKING PHONE!

My wife makes our bed
Feel so warm and smell so good
Leave at 4AM?

New York's switch is on
Ready to make some money
Wait, forgot my mask

Ubers have returned
Barely earn minimum wage
A sweatshop on wheels

For $20
Mr. George Floyd is murdered
Copper gets 20?

Tumeric Water
Fuels Cabbie's marathon shift
Is *this* all there is?

A Cabbie for Decades
"Wow, You must have seen it all"
Want to see much more

Summer 2020
Gonna go out to Coney
Can I bring a friend?

I got me a wife
10-year-old bottle of Scotch
Which do I need more?

Can't live without you
For you I cook chicken stew
And avoid Trump flu

Salad green, orange, red
This cab may be yellow but
I ain't no chicken

5AM N Train
Subway Showers overnight
My fart just hangs there

Part-time Ubers ride
Down Broadway past old Cabbie
Greek coffee food cart

Helicopter hovers
Deafening on dark Broadway
Greenwich Village tears

Half-filled apartments
Our Washington Place neighbor
Is dead, but not gone

Reconciliation?
Lunch with Trump voting cousin
Blow the damn bridge up

Corona sickness strikes me
Not getting the normal shower
Aroma can't get worse

Afraid to go out
Cannot let anyone know me
Please hide me

Corona still lingers
Most businesses remain closed
Ghostly Bronx Town Mall

New York to across Africa
Streets filled with masked protestors
Unjust killing of black lives

I am a corona survivor
It is great to be alive
This is not a hoax

Eating less meat
Buying more vegetation and fruits
Post corona healthy life

5 Train in the Bronx
October leaves falling on open cut tracks
Slow slippery ride when wet

Everything at risk
Social distance safety on long lines
Making my vote count

Yay, the bully is gone
May I please get an Amen
It's fumigation time

Alando McIntyre joined the Worker Writers School as a cashier at Golden Krust Bakery. After earning his BA in accounting from CUNY Baruch College, he now works as a humanities teacher at Success Academy in New York. McIntyre has read his poems at the Nuyorican Poets Café, PEN World Voices Festival, and elsewhere. Born in Kingston, Jamaica, he currently resides in Brooklyn.

Alfreda Small worked as a home health aide and a police administrative aide prior to her recent retirement. She is a member of District Council 37, the largest public employee union in New York City. Small earned a bachelor's degree from York College in Queens. She has read her poems at the PEN World Voices Festival and Berl's Brooklyn Poetry Shop. She currently lives in Staten Island.

Christine Yvette Lewis is a leader, organizer, and Secretary/Cultural Outreach Coordinator with Domestic Workers United (DWU), where she encourages culture and art as strongholds in the work for social justice and domestic workers' rights. As a worker-leader and multidisciplinary performance artist, Lewis has pulled from her Calypsonian roots and skills as a steel-drum player, spoken word artist, and poet to get her message out and build power. She has spoken out on initiatives like the Domestic Workers' Bill of Rights at public venues like The Colbert Report. For eight years, she has helped organize a partnership between DWU members and the Public Theater's Public Works productions of Shakespeare in the Park. She has been an active member in the Worker Writers School since its inception in 2011.

Davidson Garrett was born in Shreveport, Louisiana. In addition to driving a taxi for nearly 40 years, he has worked as an actor, Catholic elementary school teacher, waiter, apartment cleaner, bike messenger, and a clown in the Sears & Roebuck's parking lot. He is a member of SAG/AFTRA and a former member of the New York Taxi Workers Alliance. Garrett has a B.A. from the Center for Worker Education at the City College of New York and an M.S. in Education from City College. Widely published in journals and anthologies, he is author of two poetry collections, *King Lear of the Taxi* (Advent Purple Press, 2006) and *Arias of a Rhapsodic Spirit* (Kelsay Books, 2020).

Doreen McGill is a New York State licensed daycare provider and member of Domestic Workers United. She holds an associate degree in travel and tourism from Taylor Business Institute. Doreen has been active in the Worker Writers School for six years. She read her poems at the PEN World Voices Festival, WBAI, and other venues. She lives in the Chelsea neighborhood in Manhattan.

Nelson Estabon Chimilio was born and raised in the South Bronx. He has spent the majority of his life in service to community and youth development with over thirty years of experience in non-profit service, community arts, workshop facilitation, and professional development. Nelson is currently working at Phipps Neighborhood as an Assistant Program Director for the Sonia Sotomayor Community Center. Nelson has a B.A. in Theater and Communications. He has performed at Carnegie Hall, Lincoln Center, Nuyorican Poets Café, HERE Arts Center, and National Black Theatre. These coronavirus haiku are his first published poems.

Kelebohile Nkhereanye (Kele) is a food street vendor, food justice activist, community chef, and community leader in East New York. She is an immigrant from Lesotho, Southern Africa, where she learned the value of street vendors as opportunities toward economic empowerment. Currently, Nkhereanye is a retired Station Agent for NYCTA and Brooklyn Community Board 5 Board Member-Co-Chair of Parks, Sanitation, & Environment, founder of Soil Afrika Global, Inc. She is a committed member of the Street Vendor Project. Nkhereanye graduated from MCNY (Master of Public Administration), Hunter College (Sociology and Women's Studies), and New York College of Technology with AA (Hospitality Management). She has read at the PEN World Voices Festival, Nuyorican Poet Café, Union Square Farmer's Market, and Berl's Brooklyn Poetry Shop.

Kerl Brooks is a member of Domestic Workers United. She has worked as a code enforcement officer, meter reader, nursery school teacher, nanny, and home health aide. Originally from San Fernando, Trinidad and Tobago, she currently resides in Castroville, Texas.

Lorraine Garnett is a nanny in Brooklyn. She has previously worked as a preschool teacher, after school supervisor, and summer camp activities director. Her poems are forthcoming in several anthologies including *Good Cop/ Bad Cop* (Flowersong Press) and *I Can't Breathe: Poetic Anthology of Fresh Air* (Kistrech Poetry). She has read her poems at venues including the Workers United Film Festival, Berl's Brooklyn Poetry Shop, and the Crush Reading Series at Woodbine. Born and raised in Jamaica, Garnett currently lives in Brooklyn.

Nimfa Despabiladeras was born in the town of Bacon, Sorsogon City, Philippines and raised in Manilla. She currently lives in New York City where she has worked as a caregiver and housekeeper since 1997. Despabiladeras is a member of Damayan Migrant Workers Association. She has read her poems at the PEN World Voices Festival and Berl's Brooklyn Poetry Bookshop.

Paloma Zapata is a visual artist from Brooklyn. She has worked as a dog walker, retail worker, and union organizer with the Retail Action Project. Zapata has read her poems at The Green Space (with Sonia Sanchez and members of the Worker Writers School) and the PEN World Voices Festival.

Seth Goldman was born in East New York and raised in Rosedale, Queens. He has a bachelor's degree from City College. For two years in the early 1990s he worked as junior high school English teacher, but has spent most of the past four decades as a taxi driver. A member of the New York Taxi Workers Alliance, Goldman has read his poems at the PEN World Voices Festival, Berl's Brooklyn Poetry Shop, Nuyorican Poets Café, WBAI, and elsewhere.

Thomas Barzey was born and raised in the Bronx, where he still resides. He holds a B.S. in Criminal Justice from Mercy College. Barzey has worked as an office assistant, stage manager, home health aide, and currently is an actor with the Public Theatre. He has performed his poems at the People's Forum, Parachute Literary Arts' celebration of Walt Whitman's 100th birthday on Coney Island, Berl's Brooklyn Poetry Shop, and elsewhere.

Juana I, by Ana Arzoumanian, translated by Gabriel Amor

Waveform, by Amber DiPietra and Denise Leto

Style, by Dolores Dorantes, translated by Jen Hofer

PQRS, by Patrick Durgin

The Pine-Woods Notebook, by Craig Dworkin

Propagation, by Laura Elrick

Tarnac, a preparatory act, by Jean-Marie Gleize, translated by Joshua Clover with Abigail Lang and Bonnie Roy

Heiroglyphs of the Inverted World, by Rob Halpern

The Chilean Flag, by Elvira Hernández, translated by Alec Schumacher

título / title, by Legna Rodríguez Iglesias, translated by Katherine M. Hedeen

Stage Fright: Selected Plays from San Francisco Poets Theater, by Kevin Killian

The Kenning Anthology of Poets Theater: 1945-1985, edited by Kevin Killian and David Brazil

The Grand Complication, by Devin King

There Three, by Devin King

Insomnia and the Aunt, by Tan Lin

Dream of Europe: selected seminars and interviews: 1984-1992, by Audre Lorde, edited by Mayra Rodríguez Castro

The Compleat Purge, by Trisha Low

Ambient Parking Lot, by Pamela Lu

Some Math, by Bill Luoma

Partisan of Things, by Francis Ponge, translated by Joshua Corey and Jean-Luc Garneau

Festivals of Patience: The Verse Poems of Arthur Rimbaud, by Arthur Rimbaud, translated by Brian Kim Stefans

The Dirty Text, by Soleida Ríos, translated by Barbara Jamison and Olivia Lott

The Pink, by Kyle Schlesinger

Several Rotations, by Jesse Seldess

Left Having, by Jesse Seldess

Who Opens, by Jesse Seldess

Grenade in Mouth: Some Poems of Miyó Vestrini, edited by Faride Mereb and translated by Anne Boyer and Cassandra Gillig

Hannah Weiner's Open House, by Hannah Weiner, edited by Patrick Durgin

KENNING EDITIONS NFP IS A 501 (C) (3), NON-PROFIT PUBLIC CHARITY"
AND CONTRIBUTIONS ARE TAX DEDUCTIBLE.

KENNINGEDITIONS.COM